International Edition

MY PALS ARE HERE!

Science

2A

Ling Yuan

Marshall Cavendish
Education

Preface

MY PALS ARE HERE! Science follows an instructional pathway of:

- **learning** through visual lessons and guided discovery
- **developing** concepts and skills in tandem through extensive use of process skills
- **consolidating** knowledge and understanding through scaffolded instruction and practice

MY PALS ARE HERE! Science has been designed to facilitate the teaching of Science through an adaptation of the *BSCS 5E Instructional Model*, which has been widely acclaimed as one of the most effective instructional strategies in Science education.

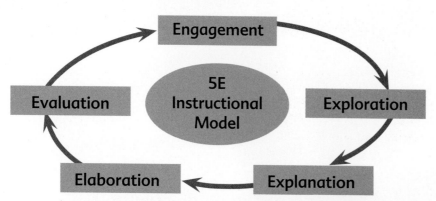

The following pages show how **MY PALS ARE HERE!** Science has been designed to support teaching Science using the *BSCS 5E Instructional Model*.

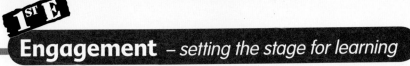

Engagement – *setting the stage for learning*

The **unit opener** introduces pupils to the topic and gives them a peek at how Science is a part of their daily lives.

These questions allow teachers to assess pupils' prior knowledge and to note any misconceptions about the topic.

3 Plants

Let's find out:
- Where can we find plants?
- How are plants different?
- What plants are useful?
- What plants are harmful?

Can you name any of the plants in your garden?

How are they different?

Plants 33

Lively and engaging visuals based on a multi-sensory approach are presented so as to stimulate interest and spur thinking.

Where do you see plants?

Why are they called land plants?

Word bank
ground • building • tree

My Scrapbook
Collect five different leaves. Place them under thin pieces of paper. Rub over them with crayons. Cut out these shapes and paste them in your scrapbook.

Vines can grow on buildings.

Can they grow on water?

bird's nest fern

vines

rose

crocus

sunflower

Teaching points:
- Have pupils recall that plants are living things so they need a place to live.
- Have pupils discuss the different places where plants grow.
- Guide pupils to observe that land plants can be found in different places. E.g. on the ground, around other plants.

34 Unit 3

Plants 35

Exploration – *developing concepts through hands-on activities*

Specially-designed visuals, rich in Science content, allow pupils to explore and discover scientific concepts in familiar contexts.

Trigger questions guide pupils in their thinking process, and help them to uncover concepts and explore connections.

Sidebar features in the Textbook, as well as the exercises in the Activity Book, provide many opportunities for experiential learning through hands-on activities, enabling pupils to gain an appreciation and deeper understanding of the concepts learnt.

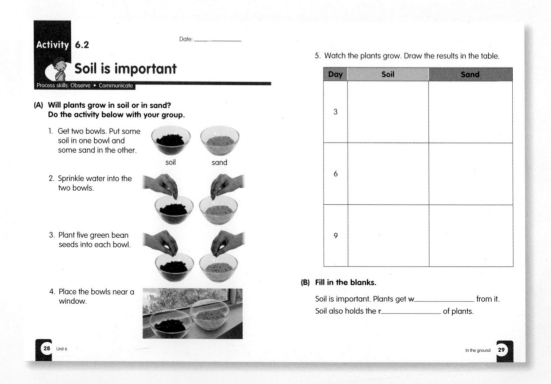

Explanation – *communicating and checking understanding*

Word bank and **labels** equip pupils with the vocabulary to discuss and communicate their thoughts and answers to the trigger questions.

Teaching points help teachers to facilitate pupils' discovery and understanding of key concepts.

Scientific concepts uncovered earlier by pupils are consolidated in the Textbook.

The purposeful use of visuals and info-graphics allows pupils of all ability levels to grasp the scientific concepts, hence building learner confidence.

Elaboration – *applying concepts in context and extending understanding*

Activities in the sidebar features and the Activity Book allow pupils to apply their knowledge and to extend their learning.

Theme pages connect scientific ideas across various topics to help pupils develop a broad-based understanding of the world around them.

5ᵀᴴ E
Evaluation – *summing up meaningfully*

At a glance is a pictorial concept map that summarises and links all the 'big ideas' dealt with in the unit.

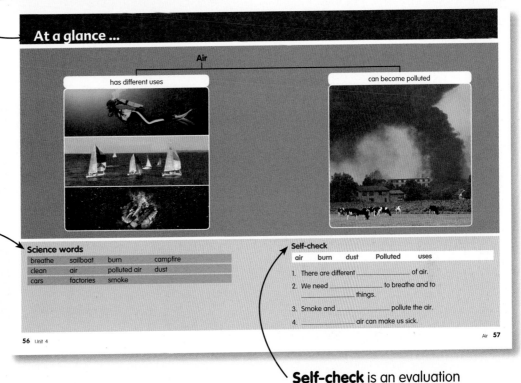

At a glance ...

Air

has different uses

can become polluted

Science words
is a list of the scientific vocabulary used in the unit.

Science words

breathe	sailboat	burn	campfire
clean	air	polluted air	dust
cars	factories	smoke	

Self-check

air	burn	dust	Polluted	uses

1. There are different _____ of air.
2. We need _____ to breathe and to _____ things.
3. Smoke and _____ pollute the air.
4. _____ air can make us sick.

56 Unit 4

Air 57

Self-check is an evaluation exercise that lets teachers informally assess pupils' understanding of the concepts taught in the unit.

Review units in the Activity Book provide for formal assessment and revision.

Date: _____

Review 1 for Units 1 – 4

(A) Choose the correct answer. Circle A, B, C or D.

1. We use our _____ to breathe.

    (A) bones   (B) muscles

    (C) lungs   (D) skeleton

2. Our heart pumps _____ to the rest of our body.

    (A) blood   (B) balloons

    (C) muscles   (D) flowers

3. An eel lives in the _____.

    (A) desert   (B) forest

    (C) pond   (D) sea

4. A snake uses its _____ to move.

    (A) body   (B) feet

    (C) tail   (D) wings

5. Which plant grows in water?

    (A) Banyan tree   (B) Bird's nest fern

    (C) Cattail   (D) Sunflower plant

6. Which fruit is <u>not</u> safe to eat?

    (A) Banana   (B) Holly berry

    (C) Papaya   (D) Pineapple

7. _____ can dirty the air.

    (A) Bicycles   (B) Factories

    (C) Trees   (D) Walking

20 Review 1

Units 1 – 4 21

Contents

Learning objectives

Learning objectives	Theme
Know the different parts in our body. Understand that the skeleton supports the body and gives the body shape. Understand that muscles help us move. Understand that our heart pumps blood to all parts of our body and that blood carries food, water and air to all parts of our body. Understand how we breathe. Understand what happens to food after we eat it. Know that a large part of our body is made up of water.	Systems
Recognise different kinds of habitats that animals live in.	Diversity
Identify characteristics of animals that enable them to survive in their habitats.	Interactions
Identify useful animals and understand why they are useful. Identify harmful animals and understand why they are harmful.	Diversity
Recognise different kinds of habitats that plants live in. Identify useful plants and understand why they are useful. Identify harmful plants and understand why they are harmful.	Diversity
Recognise the different uses of air.	Diversity
Know what wind is and what its uses are. Recognise that air is needed for burning.	Interactions
Distinguish between clean air and polluted air.	Diversity
Recognise that water can exist in different states.	Cycles, Diversity
Observe what happens when some substances are mixed with water.	Interactions
Understand that there are many objects around us that are made of rock. Classify rocks according to their size, shape, colour, pattern, texture and hardness.	Diversity
Understand the importance of soil.	Interactions
Recognise that the Sun rises in the morning and sets in the evening. Recognise the observable shapes of the Moon.	Cycles
Know that there are different star patterns in the sky.	Diversity
Know the four seasons.	Cycles
Observe and describe weather conditions associated with each season.	Diversity
Understand how seasons affect us, in terms of how we dress and the kinds of activities that we can do.	Interactions

My wonderful body

Let's find out:
- What are the different parts in our body?
- What do these body parts do?

Can you name some body parts?

How do these body parts help you?

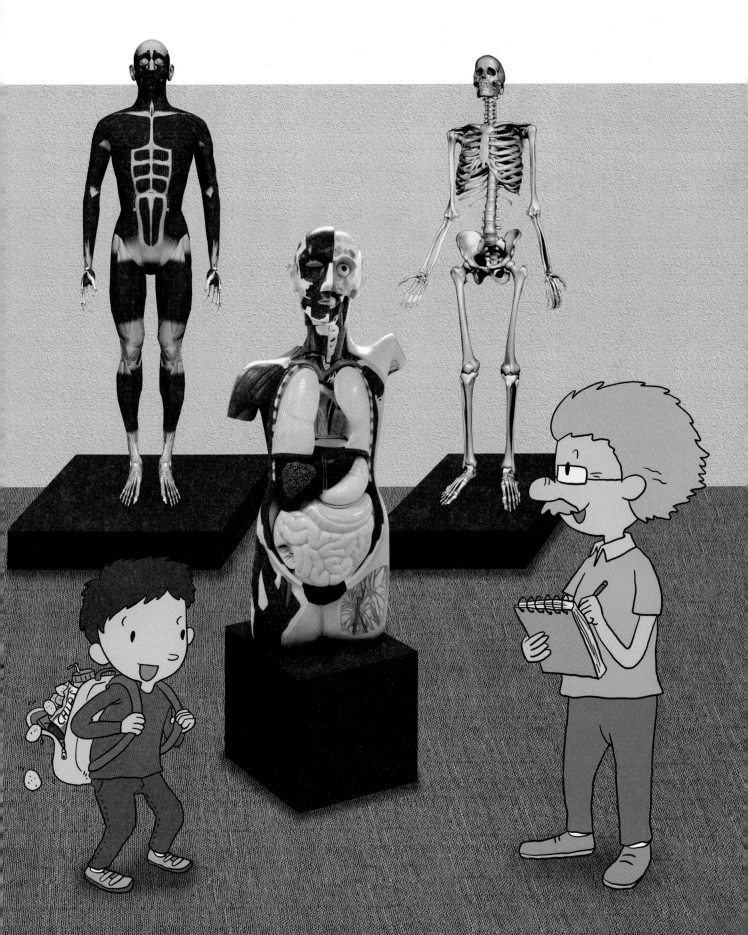

Why is Joe's hand on his chest?

What can he feel?

How do you know Zoe has had enough to eat?

Word bank

stomach • heart •
heartbeat • skeleton

Be Careful

If you eat too much during a meal, you will get a stomach ache.

zZZ

Teaching points:
- Have pupils recall that there are many parts in our body.
- Flex your arm. Get pupils to understand that your muscles and bones enable you to do this.
- Have pupils put their hands on their chest to feel their heartbeat. Then ask them to run on the spot for a minute and feel their heartbeat again. Ask if their heart is beating faster now.
- Ask pupils what they think happens to the food they eat.

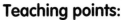

Our body is made up of many parts.

Our **skeleton supports** our body and gives the body its **shape**. Our skeleton is made up of **bones**.

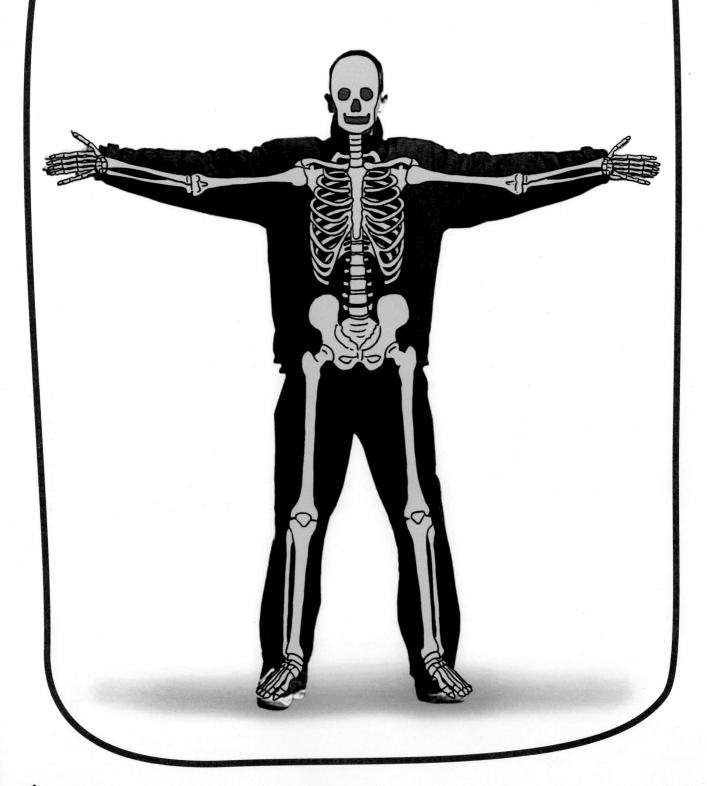

Our **muscles** and bones help us to **move** our body.

Our **heart pumps blood** through our body. The blood carries **food**, **water** and **oxygen**.

The parts of our body work together.

Our **nose**, **mouth** and **lungs** work together to help us **breathe**.

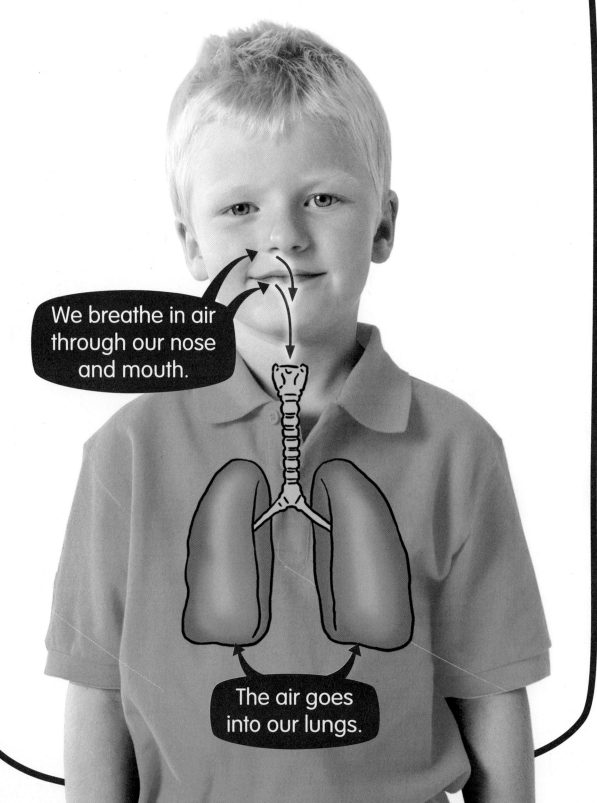

Our **stomach** and **small intestines** work together to **break down the food** we eat.

Food is broken down into smaller pieces when we chew.

Food is broken down in the stomach.

Food is further broken down and taken in by the small intestines.

Activities 1.1 and 1.2

Body parts

Our skeleton supports our body and gives our body shape.

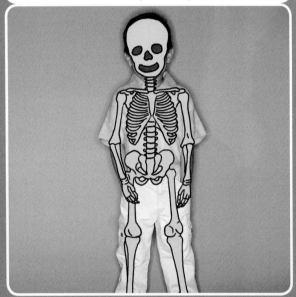

Our muscles and bones help us move.

Science words

skeleton	bones	shape
muscles	move	
heart	heartbeat	pumps blood
lungs	breathe	
stomach	small intestines	break down food

Our heart pumps blood to the rest of our body.

Our lungs help us breathe.

Our stomach and small intestines break down the food we eat.

Self-check

move	breathe	skeleton	stomach	heart

1. Our _____ is made up of bones, supports our body and gives our body shape.

2. Our muscles and bones help us _____.

3. Our _____ pumps blood.

4. Our mouth, nose and lungs work together to help us _____.

5. Our _____ and small intestines work together to break down the food we eat.

2 Amazing animals!

Let's find out:
- Where do animals live?
- How are animals different?
- What animals are useful?
- What animals are harmful?

Where do you live?

What animals visit your home?

What animals can you see?
Where do these animals live?

This butterfly likes flowers very much.

butterfly

bee

Science at home

Make your own ants' tunnel. Ask an adult to help you. Put some agar powder into a clear container. Pour hot water into it. Stir the mixture and let the agar set. Catch a few ants and place them inside. Add some sugar for their food. Cover the container and poke a few holes on the lid. The ants now have a new home.

Teaching points:
• Have pupils understand that all animals need a home.
• Have pupils identify the different animals that are in the garden, the pond and the soil.
• Guide pupils to observe how these homes are different from one another.
• Discuss the special features that help animals survive in their habitat.

snake

flowerpecker

Wow!
Orang utans are smart animals.
They can use leaves as umbrellas,
or cups to drink water.

chameleon

What animals can you see?

Where do these animals live?

How do these animals move?

gibbon

orang utan

Word bank

trees • forest • fly • glide
• climb • swing • crawl

Use both sides of paper
to save the trees in the
forest. Help protect the
home of many animals.

Teaching points:
- Have pupils identify the animals that live in trees.
- Let pupils know that the forest is the home of many animals.
- Guide pupils to understand that these animals have special features that allow them to survive in their habitat.

Where do these animals live?

Is this place hot or cold?

Where do the animals stay to keep cool?

Where can we rest?

Let's rest beside that rock over there.

kangaroo rat

Word bank

desert • bury • hide • sand • rocks

Explore

Food and water are difficult to find in the desert. How do these animals eat and drink?

Teaching points:
- Have pupils identify the animals that live in the desert.
- Tell pupils that the desert can be very hot during the day and very cold during the night.
- Tell pupils about the special features of desert animals. E.g. Kangaroo rats have pouches on their cheeks to store food.
- Discuss how these animals keep cool in the desert.

sea turtle

shark

fish

eel

What animals can you see?

Where do these animals live?

What do they use to move?

dugong

Wow!
Dugongs are called 'sea cows' because they eat water plants six to eight hours a day.

Word bank
sea • water • fins • tails • flippers

My Scrapbook

Choose a place where animals live. Then, make up an animal that can live in that place. Draw your animal and show it to your friends.

Teaching points:
- Have pupils identify the animals that live in the water.
- Let pupils know that the sea is the home of many animals.
- Guide pupils to understand that sea animals have features to help them survive in their habitat. E.g. Fish have fins to swim. They can also breathe underwater.

Animals are different.

Animals live in different places or **habitats**. Animals find **food, water** and **shelter** in their habitats.

Many animals live in the **garden**. Some of them swim in the **pond**. Some of them live in the **soil**.

Animals move in different ways. They use different **body parts** to move.

➡ Ducks have webbed feet to swim in the pond.

➡ Earthworms have no feet. They use their bodies to glide on the ground.

Many animals live in the **forest**.
Their body parts help them move in the trees.

← Birds have wings to fly.

↑ Monkeys swing from tree to tree with their arms and tails.

Animals are special.

Many animals live in the **desert**.
The desert is a hot place with little food and water.
The animals there have special body parts.

⬆ Camels have
humps to store fats.

⬇ Jackrabbits' ears
keep them cool.

⬇ Geckos can break their
tails when in danger.

Many animals live in the **sea**.
Their body parts help them move in the water.

← Fish have fins to swim.

➡ Sea turtles swim with
their flippers.

Activities 2.1 and 2.2

goat

horse

hen

rat

Which animals give us food?
Which animal does work for us?
Which animals are harmful?

 **Word bank**

milk • meat • eggs •
bite • sting •
spread diseases

Be Careful

Mosquitoes can make you sick. Apply insect repellent before going out.

cow

Don't let mosquitoes bite you!

Ouch!

mosquito

Teaching points:
- Have pupils list the food they eat and its sources.
- Guide pupils to identify useful animals.
- Let pupils discuss how some animals are useful to man. E.g. They provide food, help us work and can be our pets.
- Guide pupils to understand that some animals are harmful to man. E.g. They bite, sting and spread diseases.

Some animals are useful.

Some animals **give us food**.

↑ Hens give us eggs.

↑ Cows give us milk.

Some animals **help us work**.

⬇ Water buffaloes help us in farming.

Others are **good pets**.

⬇ Rabbits can live with us at home.

Some animals are harmful.

Some animals **bite us**.

⬇ Mosquitoes spread diseases.

Some animals **carry germs**.

⬇ Rats and cockroaches make us sick.

Activity 2.3

At a glance ...

Animals

live in different habitats

have different body parts

Science words

habitat	garden	soil	pond	forest	desert	sea
body parts	webbed feet		humps	ears	flippers	
useful	give food		help us work		good pets	
harmful	bite		carry germs			

can be useful	can be harmful

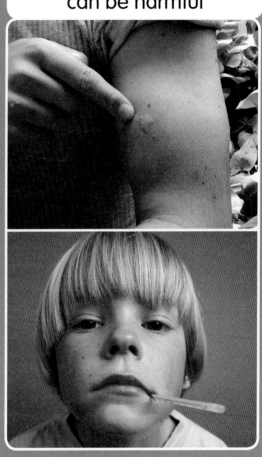

Self-check

body parts	habitats	harmful	useful

1. Animals live in different _____.

2. The animals' _____ help them survive in their habitat.

3. Some animals are _____. They give us food, help us work and are good pets.

4. Some animals are _____. They bite, sting and spread diseases.

3 Plants

Let's find out:
- Where can we find plants?
- How are plants different?
- What plants are useful?
- What plants are harmful?

Can you name any of the plants in your garden?

How are they different?

Where do you see plants?

Why are they called land plants?

bird's nest fern

rose

sunflower

ground • building • tree

My Scrapbook

Collect five different leaves. Place them under thin pieces of paper. Rub over them with crayons. Cut out these shapes and paste them in your scrapbook.

Teaching points:
- Have pupils recall that plants are living things so they need a place to live.
- Have pupils discuss the different places where plants grow.
- Guide pupils to observe that land plants can be found in different places. E.g. on the ground, around other plants.

What plants do you see?

Where do they grow?

Can these plants grow on land?

duckweed

cattail

Word bank

water plants • underwater • float

we Care

Plants also need clean, fresh water like we do. Keep ponds and lakes clean so plants will grow.

Teaching points:
- Have pupils name these plants and classify them as water plants.
- Guide pupils to observe that some water plants grow underwater and some float on the water.
- Help pupils understand the difference between land plants and water plants.

Plants grow in different places.

Plants grow in a habitat.
They get **water** and **sunlight** in their habitat.

Some plants grow on land.
They are **land plants**.

⬇ Some land plants grow on the ground.

⬇ Others grow up trees and buildings.

↓ Cacti live in the desert.
They store water in their stems.

Some plants grow in water.
They are **water plants**.

↓ Some water plants float
on the water.

↓ Others grow underwater.

Activity 3.1

What fruits and vegetables do you see?

Are all plants useful?

Which plants are harmful?

pong pong tree

Don't eat that!

weed

orchid

hibiscus

 **Word bank**

shade • beautify • food • poisonous • ill

Explore

The coconut tree is known as the 'Tree of Life'. Why?

Be Careful

Do not eat or put a part of any plant into your mouth. Not all plants are good for you.

Teaching points:
• Have pupils identify the fruits and vegetables we can eat.
• Have pupils share ideas on the other uses of plants.
• Guide pupils to understand why some plants are harmful.

Some plants are useful.

Some plants give us **fruits** and **vegetables**.

Big trees give us **shade** from the sun.

Plants can make a place look beautiful.

Some plants are harmful.

Some plants are **poisonous**.

⬇Poison ivy gives you rashes.

⬇Pong pong seeds make you very ill.

Some plants **hurt** us when we touch them.

Activity 3.2

At a glance ...

Plants

grow in different places

Science words

land plants	ground	trees	buildings
water plants	float	underwater	
fruits	vegetables	shade	
poisonous	hurt	rashes	

can be useful

can be harmful

Self-check

land   useful   places   poisonous   underwater

1. Different plants grow in different _____.
2. _____ plants grow on the ground, on buildings or on other plants.
3. Water plants float on the water or grow _____.
4. Some plants are _____. They give us food and shade, and make a place look beautiful.
5. Harmful plants can be _____ or can hurt us.

4 Air

Let's find out:

- What are the uses of air?
- What is the difference between clean and polluted air?

Can you see air?

Where is air found?

sailboat

It's very windy today.

air tank

diver

What helps the diver breathe underwater?

What helps the sailboat move?

Word bank
air • wind

Explore
Take a straw and blow into a glass of water. What do you see?

Science at home
Place a candle on a plate. Ask an adult to help you light the candle. Then, cover the candle with a glass. What happens?

campfire

Air has different uses.

We need air to **breathe**.

⬆ A diver and an astronaut also need air to breathe.

Some things need to be filled with air to work.

Sailboats need **wind** to move.
Wind is moving air.

Air is needed for **burning**.

Activity 4.1

Why do the children want to go the other way?

Why is the air around the factories dirty?

Which place looks cleaner?

factories

rubbish

bicycle

cars

 **Word bank**

clean air • polluted air • smoke • dust

Science at home

Watch cars pass by your house. Count the number of cars with only one person inside. How many cars could one bus replace?

Teaching points:
- Guide pupils to observe the difference between clean air and polluted air.
- Let pupils discuss the causes of polluted air.
- Encourage pupils to think of ways to keep the air clean and its benefits.

Polluted air is dirty and harmful.

Smoke and **dust** dirty the air.
They come from cars and factories.

Do not breathe in polluted air.
It can make you sick.

We must keep the air clean.

Walk or ride your bike.

Take the bus.

Plant more trees.

Activity 4.2

At a glance ...

Air

has different uses

Science words

breathe	sailboat	burn	campfire
clean	air	polluted air	dust
cars	factories	smoke	

can become polluted

Self-check

| air | burn | dust | polluted | uses |

1. There are different _____ of air.

2. We need _____ to breathe and to _____ things.

3. Smoke and _____ pollute the air.

4. _____ air can make us sick.

5 Water

Let's find out:
- What are the different forms of water?
- What happens when we mix water with some things?

How do you use water at home?

How much water should you drink in a day?

Where can you see water?

How is each form of water different?

Teaching points:
- Have pupils recall that water is all around us.
- Guide pupils to understand that water comes in three different forms – ice, water and steam.

Water comes in different forms.

All forms of water have **no colour**, **no smell** and **no taste**.

Ice is **cold** and **hard**.

Water **takes the shape** of its container.

Steam is **hot**. It does not have a shape.

Activity 5.1

oil

pebbles

syrup

Wow! The oil is on top of the water!

Can all things mix with water?

Which things float?

Which things sink?

Science at home

Look for different things
you can find at home, such
as sugar, salt, paint, soil,
oil, and so on. Get a few
cups of water and a spoon.
Mix each thing with each
cup of water. Which thing
disappears? Which thing
changes colour? Which
thing floats? Which thing
sinks?

sugar

Teaching points:
- Have pupils identify the substance that
  dissolves, that does not dissolve, that
  floats and that sinks.
- Ask pupils what happened to the
  substance that dissolved.

What happens when things are mixed with water?

Some things **mix together** with water and **disappear**.

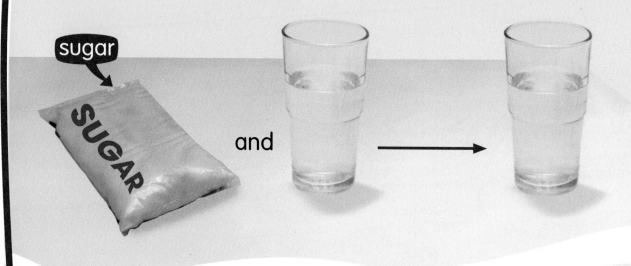

sugar

and

Some things **mix together** with water and **change colour**.

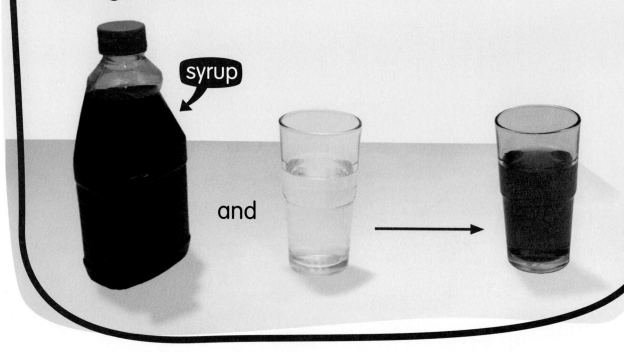

syrup

and

Some things **do not mix** with water.
They **float** on water.

oil

and

Some things do not **mix with water**.
They **sink** in water.

sand

and

Activity 5.2

At a glance ...

Water

comes in different forms

Science words

water	ice	steam	
no colour	no smell	no taste	
cold	hard	shape	hot
mix together	disappear	change colour	
do not mix	float	sink	

mixes with some things	does not mix with some things

Self-check

disappear	sink	forms

1. Water comes in different _____.

2. Water mixes together with some things. These things will _____ or change colour.

3. Water does not mix with some things. These things will float or _____.

6 In the ground

Let's find out:
- How are rocks different?
- What things are made of rock?
- Why is soil important?

What do you see on the ground?

Which rocks are big? Which ones are small?

What are the colours of the rocks?

What things are made of rock?

Like her diamond necklace!

necklace

earrings

 **Word bank**

black • red • grey • brown

Explore

Pick up five rocks around your house. Feel them with your hands. Which rocks are rough? Which ones are smooth?

 **My treasure chest**

Find a small, smooth rock. Wash it clean and paint it. You have made a rock paperweight.

Teaching points:
- Guide pupils to see that rocks have different shapes, sizes, textures and colours.
- Discuss why rocks are useful to man. E.g. We use rocks to build roads.

Rocks are different.

Rocks come in different **sizes** and **shapes**.

← Some are big.

↑ Some are small.

Rocks come in different **colours** and **patterns**.

Rocks have different **textures**.

↓ Some are smooth.

↓ Some are rough.

Some rocks are **harder** than others.

➡ Limestone is a hard rock. It was used to build the Great Pyramid of Giza.

Rocks are everywhere.

Rocks are found in the ground, in oceans, mountains and caves.

Rocks have many uses.

➜ For buildings

For roads and bridges

For statues

For jewellery

Activity 6.1

What do plants need to grow?

Where does water go when you water the plant?

Which part of the plant is in the soil?

The sand here looks and feels different from soil.

sand

spade

Be Careful

Wash your hands with soap and water after touching soil.

Teaching points:
- Have pupils recall the parts of a plant and what plants need to grow.
- Tell pupils that like rocks, soil is found in the ground. Let pupils know that soil comes from rocks.
- Show pupils that the roots of most plants are found in the soil.
- Tell pupils that plants grow and get their nutrients from soil.
- Tell pupils that soil holds the roots of plants for support.

Soil is important.

Soil is also found in the ground.
Plants grow and animals live in the soil.

Soil is important to plants.
Plants get **water** from the soil.

Soil holds the roots of plants.
It helps plants stay in place.

Activity 6.2

At a glance ...

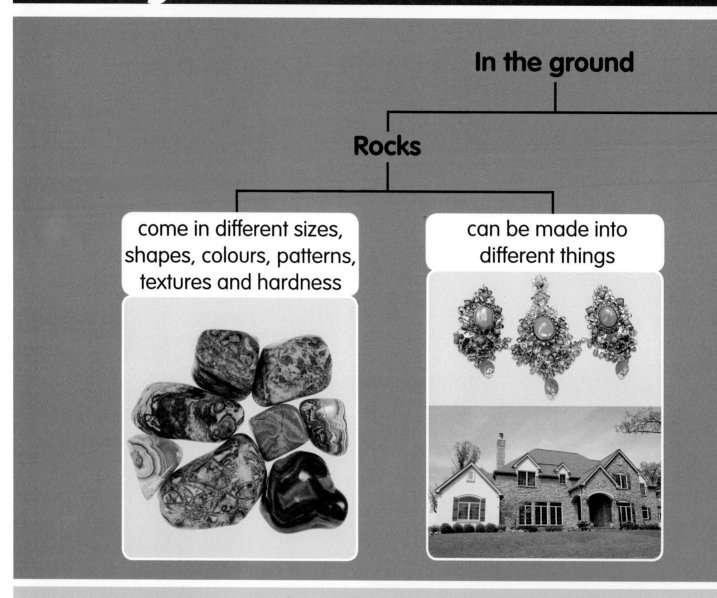

In the ground

Rocks

come in different sizes, shapes, colours, patterns, textures and hardness

can be made into different things

Science words

textures	rough	smooth	harder
patterns			
rocks	buildings	roads	bridges	statues	jewellery
soil	sand		

Soil

is important to plants

Self-check

ground   rocks   water   things

1. The _____ is made up of rocks and soil.

2. _____ come in different sizes, shapes, colours, patterns, textures and hardness.

3. Many different _____ are made of rock.

4. Soil is important to plants. Plants get _____ and support from the soil.

7 Day and night

Let's find out:
- When does the Sun rise and set?
- What are the different shapes of the Moon?
- What are the different star patterns in the sky?

Which do you like better, day or night? Why?

What time of day is it in the picture? How do you know?

When does the Sun rise?

 **Word bank**

evening • morning • set

My Scrapbook

Draw and colour a picture of the sunrise or the sunset.

Teaching points:
- Ask pupils when the Sun rises and when it sets.
- Ask pupils where in their house they can see the sunrise and the sunset from.
- Let pupils talk about the things they can do when the Sun is up and when the Sun is down.

The Sun rises and sets every day.

The **Sun rises** in the **morning** and **sets** in the **evening**.

⬆ Sunrise

⬇ Sunset

We have many day and night activities.

The Sun changes what we do.

When the Sun is up,
we study in school and play with our friends.

When the Sun is down,
we eat our dinner and go to bed.

Activity 7.1

What do you see in the sky at night?

What other shapes of the Moon have you seen?

Do you see a pattern in the stars? What do they look like?

shooting star

telescope

Look at the stars!

 **Word bank**

crescent moon • full moon
• half moon

Science at home

Draw the Moon you see in the sky every night for 29 days. What do you notice about the Moon's shape?

Teaching points:
- Tell pupils that the Moon changes its shape, and forms the crescent moon, half moon and full moon.
- Guide pupils to observe that stars can form different patterns. E.g. The star pattern Leo looks like a lion.

The Moon changes its shape.

The **Moon** can have different shapes.

Sometimes, the Moon is round.
Sometimes, we see only half of it.
At other times, we do not see the Moon at all.

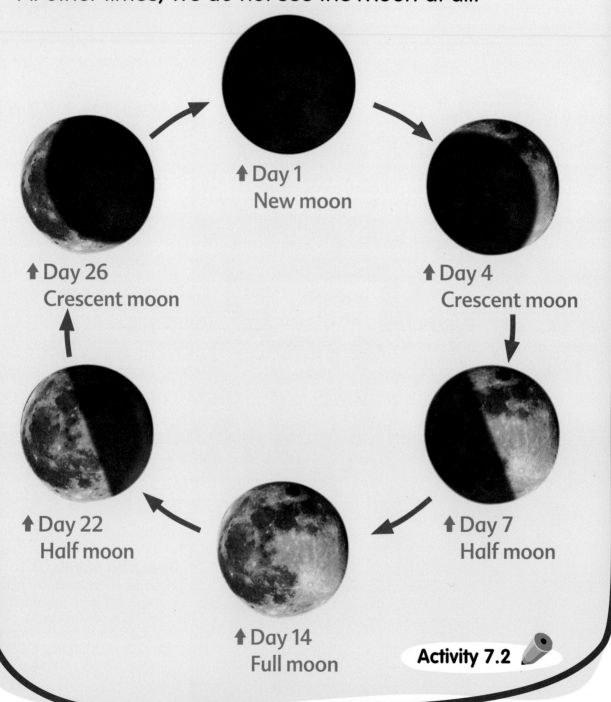

↟ Day 1
New moon

↟ Day 4
Crescent moon

↟ Day 7
Half moon

↟ Day 14
Full moon

↟ Day 22
Half moon

↟ Day 26
Crescent moon

Activity 7.2

Stars form different patterns.

A group of **stars** can form a pattern.
We see a **star pattern** if we 'connect the dots'.

There are many star patterns in the sky.
They even have names.

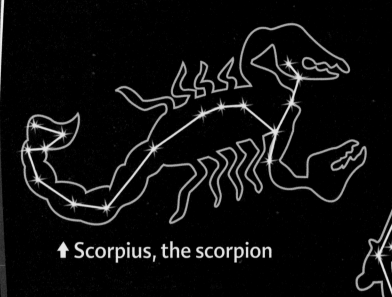

↑ Scorpius, the scorpion

→ Orion, the hunter

Activity 7.3

At a glance ...

Day and night

The Sun

rises in the morning and sets in the evening

Science words

Sun	Moon	stars
rise	set	
morning	evening	
crescent moon	half moon	full moon
star patterns		

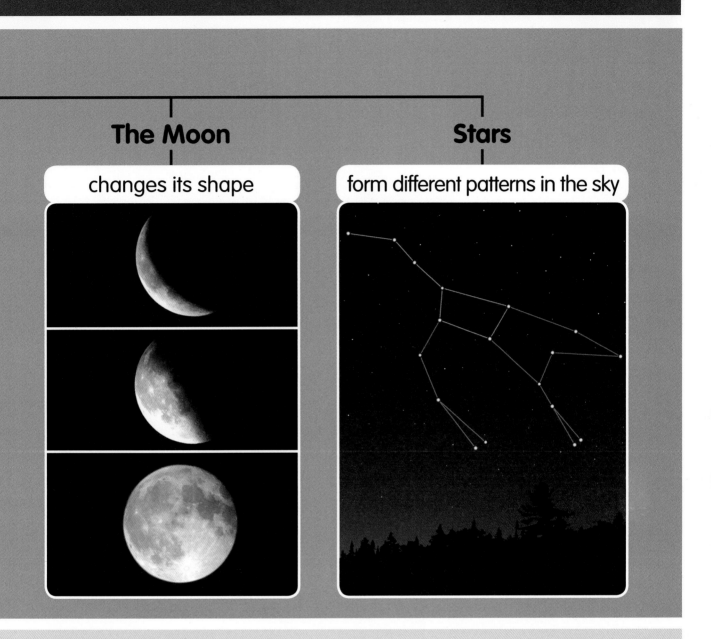

The Moon
changes its shape

Stars
form different patterns in the sky

Self-check

Moon	Stars	Sun

1. The _____ rises in the morning and sets in the evening.

2. The _____ has different shapes — the crescent moon, the half moon and the full moon.

3. _____ form different patterns in the sky.

8 The seasons

Let's find out:
- What are the four seasons?
- What is the weather like during each season?
- What do we wear during each season?
- What can we do during each season?

What is the weather like today?

Which is your favourite season? Why?

kite

T-shirt

Bermudas

Is it warm or cold during spring? How do you know?

What else can you do during spring?

Word bank

bloom

we Care

Do not pluck flowers from plants. Only pick up the ones that have fallen to the ground.

Teaching points:
- Have pupils understand that the picture depicts a typical spring day.
- Tell pupils that flowers start to bloom during spring.
- Tell pupils that in some countries, spring time also brings light rain.

wetsuit

visor

beach

vest

shorts

sandcastle

What is the weather like during summer?

Why are Joe and Dr Atom dressed like this?

Word bank

hot

Science at home

Look at the clothes you have in your wardrobe. Which ones can you wear during summer? Why?

straw hat

sunglasses

hand fan

Teaching points:
- Tell pupils that the picture depicts a typical summer day.
- Have pupils understand that Dr Atom and Joe are wearing headgear to protect their head and face from the heat.
- Ask pupils to discuss what they should not wear in hot weather and why.

Wow!
Some trees have leaves that remain green throughout the year. These trees are called evergreens.

scarf

jacket

wheelbarrow

dried leaves

What is the weather like during autumn?

What happens to trees during autumn?

coat

rake

My
Scrapbook

Place a leaf in a thick book. Close the book and check the leaf after ten days. Paste the leaf in your scrapbook and tell a friend what it looks like.

Teaching points:
- Tell pupils that the picture depicts a typical autumn day.
- Tell pupils that it is usually quite windy during autumn.
- Tell pupils that during autumn, the leaves of some trees go from green to yellow to orange to red and then to brown before they fall off, leaving the tree bare.
- Tell pupils that some animals gather food during autumn to store for later.

What is the weather like during winter?

What can you do during winter?

snowman

winter coat

Word bank

cold • snow • hibernate

Explore

Find out which animals sleep throughout winter.

Teaching points:
- Tell pupils that the picture depicts a typical winter day.
- Have pupils understand that snow is frozen water.
- Ask pupils to discuss what they should not wear in cold weather and why.
- Have pupils infer that different seasons have different weather conditions.

What is the weather like?

During **spring**, it is **warm**.

⬇ Flowers bloom during spring.

During **summer**, it is **hot**.

⬇ It is very sunny on most days.

During **autumn**, it is **cool** and **windy**.

⬇ Leaves of some trees dry up and fall to the ground.

During **winter**, it is **cold**.

⬆ Most trees are bare.

⬇ Snow falls.

Activity 8.1

Clothes and activities

During spring, we wear clothes that let us enjoy the outdoors. We cycle and fly kites.

During summer, we wear clothes that keep us cool. We swim and have barbecues.

During autumn, we wear clothes that protect us from the wind. We rake dried leaves and play with them!

During winter, we wear clothes that keep us warm. We build snowmen and ride sleds.

Activities 8.2 and 8.3

At a glance ...

Spring

Winter

There are
four seasons.

Summer

Autumn

Science words

seasons		
spring	warm	
summer	hot	
autumn	cool	windy
winter	cold	snow

Self-check

cold   cool   seasons   warm   clothes

1. There are four _____.

2. Spring is _____. We wear clothes that allow us to enjoy the outdoors. We cycle and fly kites.

3. Summer is hot. We wear clothes that keep us _____. We swim and have barbecues.

4. Autumn is cool and windy. We wear _____ that protect us from the wind. We rake dried leaves and play with them.

5. Winter is _____. We wear clothes that keep us warm. We build snowmen and ride sleds.

Acknowledgements

Front cover

lupine © Aquadaisy/Dreamstime.com; sky © Pakhnyushchyy/Dreamstime.com; squirrel © Pam Lane/iStockphoto.com; blueberries © Marlena Zagajewska/Dreamstime.com

Title page

squirrel on tree © Kimberly Wright/Dreamstime.com

Unit 1 My wonderful body

2 child © Quavondo Nguyen/iStockphoto.com; 2 – 3 background, display stands, muscle man and skeleton © Marshall Cavendish International (S) Pte Ltd; 2 digestive track © Eti Swinford/Dreamstime.com; 3 human torso © Eti Swinford /Dreamstime.com; 4 – 5 running track © Sanja Gjenero/sxc.hu; 4 – 5 picnic © New Numerals CD; 6 man © Aurimas Gudas/sxc.hu; 7 girl © Gbh007/Dreamstime.com; 7 boy © Jack Hollingsworth/Dreamstime.com; 8 boy © Redbaron/Dreamstime.com; 9 girl © Jack Hollingsworth/Dreamstime.com; 10 boy © Ron Chapple Studios/Dreamstime.com; 10 girl © Shariff Che' Lah/Dreamstime.com; 11 man © Lawrence Wee/Dreamstime.com; 11 boy © Jennifer Hogan/Dreamstime.com; 11 girl © Olga Sapegina/Dreamstime.com

Unit 2 Amazing animals!

12 child © Jupiter Images CD; 13 bed © Maksym Bondarchuk/iStockphoto.com; 14 earthworm © Bernd Lang/Dreamstime.com; 14 duck © New Numerals CD; 14 ants © Scott Harms/iStockphoto.com; 14 tadpoles © Jolanta Dabrowska/Dreamstime.com; 15 snake © Mariya Bibikova/iStockphoto.com; 15 flowerpecker © J.M.Garg (jmgarg1@gmail.com) http://en.wikipedia.org/wiki/User:Jmgarg1 *Creating Awareness of Indian Flora & Fauna*; 15 chameleon © Siwei CD; 15 orangutan © Siwei CD; 16 gibbon © Chanyut Sribua-rawd/iStockphoto.com; 18 desert user:highqueue/Wikimedia Commons/Public Domain; 18 elf owl © Siwei CD; 18 bighorn © Lisa Kyle Young/iStockphoto.com; 18 tortosie © Paul Wang/iStockphoto.com; 18 gecko © June74/Dreamstime.com; 19 kangaroo rat user:Rex/Wikimedia Commons/Public Domain; 20 sea turtle © Siwei CD; 20 shark © Andrejs Pidjass/Dreamstime.com; 20 eel © Warwick Lister-Kaye/iStockphoto.com; 21 dugong © Dejan Sarman/iStockphoto.com; 22 duck © Lidian Neeleman/Dreamstime.com; 22 earthworm © Bernd Lang/Dreamstime.com; 23 eagle © Siwei CD; 23 monkey © Rene Drouyer/Dreamstime.com; 24 camel © Riyas Hamza/sxc.hu; 24 gecko © June74/Dreamstime.com; 25 sea turtle © Siwei CD; 26 goat © Christopher Elwell/Dreamstime.com; 26 hen walking © Jetfoto/Dreamstime.com; 26 hen in nest © Dmitriy Shironosov/Dreamstime.com; 26 rat © Robert Owen-Wahl/sxc.hu; 26 rat © Kau Kuusik-Greenbaum/sxc.hu 27 cow © Christopher Elwell/Dreamstime.com; 28 hen © Jetfoto/Dreamstime.com; 28 eggs, milk © Marshall Cavendish International (S) Pte Ltd; 28 cow © Marshall Cavendish International (S) Pte Ltd; 28 water buffalo © Josef Muellek/Dreamstime.com; 28 girl with rabbit © Rod He/Dreamstime.com; 29 mosquito © Knorre/Dreamstime.com; 29 child © Adrian Hughes/Dreamstime.com; 30 camels © Siwei CD; 30 monkey © Siloto Siloto/Dreamstime.com; 30 bird © Miroslaw Piotrowski/Dreamstime.com; 30 snake © Amwu/Dreamstime.com; 30 shark © Siwei CD; 31 meat © Marshall Cavendish International (S) Pte Ltd; 31 horse carriage © Lee Torrens/Dreamstime.com; 31 mosquito bite © Simon Krzic/Dreamstime.com

Unit 3 Plants

32 child © Tracy Whiteside/iStockphoto.com; 32 gazebo © Kenn W. Kiser/sxc.hu; 34 house © Vesna Sajn/iStockphoto.com; 36 boat © Lisa Comstock/sxc.hu; 36 water hyacinth © Ronnie Bergeron/morguefile.com; 37 duckweed © xandert/morguefile.com; 37 cattail © Robert Wragg/morguefile.com; 38 trees © Ben Earwicker/sxc.hu; 38 tree with vines © Marshall Cavendish International (S) Pte Ltd; 38 house Graham Bould/Wikimedia Commons/Public Domain; 39 cactus © richd/morguefile.com; 39 water lily © Marshall Cavendish International (S) Pte Ltd; 39 hydrilla © J.M.Garg (jmgarg1@gmail.com) http://en.wikipedia.org/wiki/User:Jmgarg1 *Creating Awareness of Indian Flora & Fauna*; 40 coconut tree © Nadia Arai/sxc.hu; 41 pong pong tree © Marshall Cavendish International (S) Pte Ltd; 42 picnic US Forest Service/Wikimedia Commons/Public Domain; 42 garden © Bill Silvermintz/sxc.hu; 43 pong pong fruit © Marshall Cavendish International (S) Pte Ltd; 43 poison ivy © Nathanphoto/Dreamstime.com; 43 roses © Marshall Cavendish International (S) Pte Ltd; 43 thorn © Peter Suneson/sxc.hu; 43 cactus © Jon Sullivan/pdphoto.org; 44 house © Brian Lary/sxc.hu; 44 lily pads © mzacha/morguefile.com; 45 girl with vegetables © Trinette Reed/Dreamstime.com; 45 garden © rinhtaray/sxc.hu; 45 holly berry © Ronald Van Der Beek/Dreamstime.com; 45 girl © Calamityjohn/Dreamstime.com

Unit 4 Air

46 child © En Tien Ou/istockphoto.com; 46 kite © Joel Terrell/sxc.hu; 46 umbrella © New Numerals CD; 46 beach ball © New Numerals CD; 47 hot air balloon © Corel Photo CD; 47 boat © abcdz2000/sxc.hu; 48 sailboat © Corel Photo CD; 50 diver © Corel Photo CD; 50 astronaut © New Numerals CD; 50 balloons © Marshall Cavendish International (S) Pte Ltd; 50 football players © Siwei CD; 51 sailboats © Corel Photo CD; 51 candles and glasses © Marshall Cavendish International (S) Pte Ltd; 54 city © Yarik Mishin/sxc.hu; 54 factories © Jacus/Dreamstime.com; 54 man on bike © Monkey Business Images/Dreamstime.com; 55 boy on bike © Alexander Hafemann/iStockphoto.com; 55 girls © Monkey Business Images/Dreamstime.com; 55 school bus © James Steidl/Dreamstime.com; 55 girl with flower pots © Thomas Perkins/Dreamstime.com; 56 diver © Corel Photo CD; 56 sailboats © Michele Lorenz/sxc.hu; 56 campfire © Marshall Cavendish International (S) Pte Ltd; 57 pollution © New Numerals CD